Exercise 1 — PRONUNCIATION AND SYLLABLES I

One key to better spelling is pronunciation. When you encounter a hard-to-spell word, pronounce it syllable by syllable, so that you hear the sound made by each part of the word. Hearing the sounds will help you to spell words with problem areas, such as double letters or unstressed vowel sounds.

A syllable is a word part that is pronounced as a separate sound. Usually, there is only one vowel sound in each syllable:

day	*day*	(one syllable)
muffin	*muf/fin*	(two syllables)
location	*lo/ca/tion*	(three syllables)

If you aren't sure how to pronounce a word or divide it into syllables, check a dictionary.

DIRECTIONS: Pronounce each word syllable by syllable. As you say a syllable, write it on the blank line to the right, and put a slash mark (/) between syllables. Then cover columns 1 and 2, and write the whole word in column 3.

Example: characteristic   *char/ac/ter/is/tic*   *characteristic*

1. community
2. environment
3. liquor
4. athlete
5. institution
6. temperature
7. tomorrow
8. committed
9. different
10. privilege
11. government
12. jewelry

EXTRA PRACTICE

Make your own list of two or more words that you have trouble spelling. (Hint: Look for misspelled words in your compositions, assignments, or tests.) Divide the words on your list into syllables, and pronounce each syllable as an aid to spelling.

Answers begin on page 28.

4

■ *Exercise 2* PRONUNCIATION AND SYLLABLES II

When you spell, be careful not to leave out or add extra letters and syllables. Also be on the lookout for reversed letters such as p*erf*er for p*ref*er. To check for errors like these, read the word aloud exactly as you have written it. This way, you will "hear" spelling mistakes.

> **DIRECTIONS:** In each sentence, pronounce the underlined word *as it is written.* Is it spelled correctly? If so, write *OK.* If not, cross it out and write the correct spelling above. Pronounce the word correctly as you write it.

intelligent

Example: *Ricardo is quite ~~intelleligent~~.*

1. The bank has three <u>convient</u> locations.
2. Howard Reeves gave an excellent <u>presentatation</u>.
3. Never use tranquilizers in <u>combation</u> with alcohol.
4. Division and <u>multiplication</u> were difficult for me when I was a child.
5. That's <u>exatly</u> how I feel too.
6. Look at that <u>unususual</u> insect crawling on your salad.
7. You are <u>resposible</u> for your own belongings.
8. That question is <u>irrevelant</u>; please stick to the point.
9. Living downtown has certain <u>avdantages</u>.
10. Can you <u>explan</u> your tardiness to the principal?
11. I will not answer any questions until my <u>lawer</u> is present.
12. My brother works in a <u>libary</u>.
13. We purchased the <u>furninture</u> on the installment plan.
14. Let's hope the football team has a more <u>successful</u> season this year.
15. Katie tries to be <u>ecomical</u> when she goes shopping.

convient

presentation

Answers begin on page 28.

Exercise 3   PRONUNCIATION AND VOWELS

Many times, a vowel combination or its placement in a word can be confusing. Pronouncing the word can help to get the order right:

influential: in/flu/en/tial; quiet: qui/et

In some vowel combinations, the order of the vowels follows a pattern, even though the combination represents more than one sound:

ea: leather, real

Many times, however, you must memorize the order and placement of the vowels in a word.

> **DIRECTIONS:** In each set of words, find the misspelled word if there is one. Blacken the space in the answer grid over the number that corresponds to the misspelled word. If there is no misspelled word, blacken the space numbered (5).

Example: (1) court (2) trout (3) giudance (4) suit

1. (1) gaiety (2) villain (3) marraige (4) waive
2. (1) gauze (2) usually (3) chaulk (4) August
3. (1) trapezoid (2) paraniod (3) bunion (4) suspension
4. (1) reaserch (2) league (3) cleanser (4) aerosol
5. (1) country (2) courage (3) coupon (4) course
6. (1) tough (2) thourough (3) through (4) though
7. (1) vauge (2) valiant (3) devaluation (4) variance
8. (1) gradually (2) mutual (3) muisician (4) bruise
9. (1) launch (2) restuarant (3) guardian (4) gauge
10. (1) beutiful (2) amateur (3) bureau (4) beauty
11. (1) miniature (2) parliament (3) straight (4) aisle
12. (1) carraige (2) campaign (3) cordial (4) explanation
13. (1) pageant (2) peseant (3) present (4) pleasant
14. (1) boardroom (2) coastal (3) woarsen (4) hoarse
15. (1) biscuit (2) buisness (3) building (4) bullet

Answers begin on page 28.

■ *Exercise 4*   THE *i* + *e* COMBINATION

Follow these rules when spelling words with the *i* + *e* combination:
  The letter *i* goes before the *e*:
    friend, believe
  except after the letter *c* sounding like *see*:
    ceiling, receipt
  or when *i* + *e* sounds like *ay*:
    neighbor, weigh

There are some exceptions to the "*c* rule":
  science, species, ancient, conscience, conscientious, financier

There are also some exceptions to the general rule:
  weird, height, either, neither, foreign, sovereign, forfeit, leisure, seize

---

DIRECTIONS: In each of the following sentences, underline the incorrectly spelled *i* + *e* word. Rewrite the word on the blank, spelling it correctly. If there is no misspelled word in the sentence, write *OK* on the blank.

Example: *The chief of police gave his own* <u>*neice*</u> *a ticket.*   *niece*

1. Can you believe how much the nieghbor's dog weighs?   1. _____

2. What a releif to have leisure time with neither work nor family pressure interfering.   2. _____

3. We didn't percieve any errors on the receipt for the freight.   3. _____

4. No mischeif is allowed at the day camp; if they misbehave, the children must <u>forfeit</u> their swimming privileges.   4. _____

5. The quarterback looked down the field for a reciever.   5. _____

6. Either I have been deceived, or someone has moved a peice on the chessboard.   6. _____

7. Can you conceive of anyone so weird?   7. _____

8. Scientists' goals include ending the seiges of flu that occur in winter.   8. _____

EXTRA PRACTICE

Write one paragraph that contains all of the following words:

neighbor

believe

niece

receive

friend

Answers begin on page 28.

■ *Exercise 5* MORE SPELLING PROBLEMS

Many words are difficult to spell because they contain one or more of the following problems:

Silent letter:

gnaw (silent *g*); *descend* (silent *c*)

Double letter:

arrangement (double *r*); *possession* (double *s*, two sets)

Internal or unstressed vowel:

separate, not *seperate*

solitary, not *solatary*

Nonphonetic spelling (the word isn't spelled the same way as it is pronounced):

colonel; victual

DIRECTIONS: In each set of words, find the misspelled word if there is one. Blacken the space in the answer grid over the number that corresponds to the misspelled word. If there is no misspelled word, blacken the space numbered (5).

Example: *(1) minite (2) privilege (3) residence (4) engineer*

1. (1) curriculum (2) currious (3) circus (4) encouraging
2. (1) ache (2) acreage (3) vacate (4) vacillate
3. (1) sympathize (2) surprise (3) pleazure (4) minimize
4. (1) irrelavant (2) separate (3) dominated (4) prevalent
5. (1) diligent (2) parallel (3) fulfillment (4) intellectual
6. (1) January (2) Wednesday (3) Febuary (4) Saturday
7. (1) delegate (2) vegatable (3) permanent (4) versatile
8. (1) psychology (2) physics (3) symmetrical (4) syringe
9. (1) malign (2) gost (3) blighted (4) gnashed
10. (1) embarrass (2) acommodate (3) academy (4) necessary
11. (1) vacuum (2) perfume (3) resume (4) asume
12. (1) catalogue (2) catagory (3) magnitude (4) marathon
13. (1) morgage (2) knapsacks (3) nimbly (4) deception
14. (1) hydrant (2) analyze (3) criticyze (4) anonymous

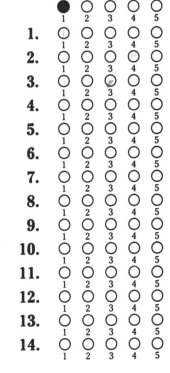

Answers begin on page 28.

Exercise 6 COMPOUNDS AND PREFIXES

When two words are joined to form a **compound word,** the spelling of each separate word is kept the same; the words are simply joined together:

door + knob = doorknob; light + hearted = lighthearted

A **prefix** is a word part added to the beginning of a word. The prefix itself is not a word, but it changes the meaning of the word to which it is added. When adding prefixes to words, keep the original spelling of the base word:

re + action = reaction; un + noticed = unnoticed

DIRECTIONS: Here are two different spelling practices. In the first column, combine the words and word parts. Then write the resulting word on the blank. In the second column, write *OK* if the word is properly spelled. If it is misspelled, spell the word correctly on the blank.

Example: *mis + spell =* misspell

1. week + end = ______
2. room + mate = ______
3. heavy + weight = ______
4. bar + room = ______
5. share + holder = ______
6. re + incarnation = ______
7. mis + manage = ______
8. pre + register = ______
9. pro + rated = ______
10. in + convenient = ______
11. un + fold = ______
12. il + legible = ______
13. super + sonic = ______
14. semi + monthly = ______
15. ir + regular = ______

Example: *sunshine* OK

1. shortstop ______
2. bookeeper ______
3. homeowner ______
4. newsstand ______
5. headsstrong ______
6. unnatural ______
7. disatisfied ______
8. imaterial ______
9. remploy ______
10. disagree ______
11. nontoxic ______
12. innedible ______
13. postdate ______
14. discharge ______
15. irelevant ______

EXTRA PRACTICE

1. Make up a list of five compound words.
2. Using a dictionary for help, make a list of ten words, one with each of these prefixes:

   re, mis, pre, in, il, ir, un, non, semi, dis

Answers begin on page 28.

Exercise 7   SUFFIXES I

A **suffix** is a word part that is added to the end of a word. Use the rules below to add the *s* suffix and other suffixes that begin with consonants: *ment, ful, less, ness,* and *ly.*

1) Add the *s* suffix and other consonant suffixes directly to most words:

   play — plays, improve — improvement, careful — carefully

2) If the word ends in *y* after a consonant (not a vowel), change *y* to *i* before adding a consonant suffix:

   beauty — beautiful, merry — merriment, penny — penniless

   When *y* is changed to *i,* the *s* ending becomes *es:*

   bully — bullies, cry — cries

3) If the word ends in *s, z, sh, ch,* or *x,* the *s* ending becomes *es* (and is pronounced as an extra syllable):

   brush — brushes, kiss — kisses, box — boxes

   Never add *'s* to make a singular noun plural or to add a verb ending:

   WRONG: *Three sandwich's*   *He try's*

   RIGHT: *Three sandwiches*   *He tries*

Note: Some words are exceptions to the rules and must be memorized:

   true — truly, argue — argument

DIRECTIONS: Here are two different spelling practices. In the first column, add the suffix to each word and write the resulting word on the blank. In the second column, write *OK* if the underlined word is correctly spelled. If it is misspelled, spell the word correctly on the blank.

Example: sandwich + s = <u>*sandwiches*</u>

1. annoy + s = _____
2. fine + ly = _____
3. blame + less = _____
4. attach + s = _____
5. fly + s = _____
6. crazy + ness = _____
7. pay + ment = _____
8. plenty + ful = _____
9. resist + s = _____
10. pain + ful + ly = _____

Example: full emploiment   <u>*employment*</u>

1. <u>talks</u> _____
2. two <u>baby's</u> _____
3. a <u>committment</u> _____
4. yours <u>truely</u> _____
5. scared <u>witless</u> _____
6. french <u>fry's</u> _____
7. an <u>arguement</u> _____
8. six <u>tests</u> _____
9. she <u>worry's</u> _____
10. he <u>watchs</u> _____

Answers begin on page 28.

■ *Exercise 8*   **SUFFIXES II**

The following rules apply to suffixes that begin with the vowels *a, e,* and *o.*
Some examples of these vowel suffixes are *able, ed, er, est,* and *ous.*

4) Add vowel suffixes like these directly to most words:
   play — played, wait — waiter, cavern — cavernous

5) If the word ends in silent *e,* drop the *e* before adding a suffix that begins
   with *a, e,* or *o:*

   adore — adorable, fame — famous

   However, keep the silent *e* after *c* or *g:*

   courage — courageous, trace — traceable

6) In one-syllable words ending in one vowel and one consonant, double the
   consonant before adding a suffix that begins with *a, e,* or *o:*

   wrap — wrapped, big — biggest, hug — huggable

   In longer words ending in one vowel and one consonant, double the
   consonant *only* if the stress is on the final syllable of the base word:

   submit — submitted (stress on final syllable)

   visit — visited (stress on first syllable)

   Note: Never double *w, y,* or *x.*

7) If the word ends in *y* after a consonant (not a vowel), change *y* to *i* before
   adding a suffix that begins with *a, e,* or *o:*

   study — studied, carry — carrier, envy — envious

DIRECTIONS: Using rules 1–7, add the vowel suffix to each word and
write the word on the blank.

Example: *deplore* + *able* = ___*deplorable*___

1. listen + er = _____

2. try + ed = _____

3. desire + able = _____

4. trap + ed = _____

5. reveal + ed = _____

6. sleepy + er = _____

7. annoy + ance = _____

8. biodegrade + able = _____

9. sloppy + est = _____

10. expel + ed = _____

11. advantage + ous = _____

12. limit + ed = _____

Answers begin on page 28.

Exercise 9   SUFFIXES III

Some suffixes begin with the letter *i*; *ing*, *ish*, and *ize* are among the most common. These suffixes, as well as the suffix *y*, follow the same rules as the other vowel suffixes with the following exceptions:

8) Always keep the letter *y* when adding a suffix that begins with *i*:

marry — marrying, thirty — thirtyish

9) Before adding *y* or a suffix beginning with *i*, drop the silent *e*, even when it follows *c* or *g*:

lace — lacy, trudge — trudging

> **DIRECTIONS:** Keeping in mind rules 1–9, look at the underlined words in each sentence. If a word is spelled correctly, write *OK* above it. If it is misspelled, cross it out and write the correction above it.

OK dropping

Example: The baby <u>loves</u> <u>droping</u> things from her high chair.

1. It <u>seemes</u> that Mrs. Huxtable is always <u>hurring.</u>
2. Derrick <u>wonderred</u> if he'd ever get over his <u>saddness.</u>
3. The <u>lady's</u> sat down and <u>daintyly</u> <u>siped</u> their tea.
4. Ron <u>returned</u> to work, thus <u>enableing</u> Sharon to go back to college.
5. I never <u>expected</u> to see my grandmother <u>walkking</u> down the street while <u>bouncing</u> a basketball.
6. Billy <u>play's</u> with his children's <u>toies</u> more than they do; he's <u>excited</u> because they just got some new <u>raceing</u> <u>car's</u>.
7. Do you <u>truely</u> believe that men are less <u>likly</u> to make a <u>committment</u> than women?
8. Heather <u>sincerly</u> <u>wishes</u> to apologize for her <u>thoughtless</u> <u>remarkes</u> yesterday; her <u>unkindness</u> was not intentional.

EXTRA PRACTICE

1. Write five things that you <u>enjoy doing</u>. Use the *ing* suffix correctly.
   Example: *swimming in the ocean*
2. Write five <u>plural</u> items that you buy at the grocery store. Use the *s* ending correctly.
   Example: *three boxes of crackers*
3. Write sentences using the <u>past tense</u> of each of these verbs:
   finish, stop, purchase, plan, work, marry, happen, commit
   Example: *John finished the exam before anyone else.*

Answers begin on page 28.

■ *Exercise 10*   SPELLING REVIEW I

> **DIRECTIONS:** In each set of words, find the misspelled word if there is one. Blacken the space in the answer grid over the number that corresponds to the misspelled word. If there is no misspelled word, blacken the space numbered (5).

Example: (1) *unattractive* (2) *unsure* (3) *unecessary* (4) *united*

1. (1) households (2) reflectively (3) driveing (4) therefore
2. (1) foundry (2) contrary (3) momentary (4) gallery
3. (1) comunity (2) comical (3) commonplace (4) commercial
4. (1) yielding (2) weighing (3) dieting (4) decieving
5. (1) suffocate (2) illustrate (3) demostrate (4) irate
6. (1) impossible (2) possess (3) tresspass (4) congress
7. (1) placement (2) squarely (3) tastey (4) ninety
8. (1) strumming (2) steaming (3) aiming (4) framing
9. (1) capatalist (2) communist (3) socialist (4) realist
10. (1) irregular (2) irrelevant (3) iritate (4) ironic
11. (1) educator (2) perpendicular (3) equater (4) tutor
12. (1) variance (2) excellence (3) defiance (4) nonsence
13. (1) portrayal (2) dutyful (3) joyous (4) swaying
14. (1) endless (2) friendship (3) cioncidence (4) really
15. (1) eveness (2) thickness (3) sadness (4) strangeness
16. (1) courageous (2) wholely (3) peaceable (4) excitement
17. (1) unnatural (2) unnoticed (3) unnending (4) undo
18. (1) physics (2) phsychology (3) psychiatrist (4) psychic
19. (1) laziness (2) storibook (3) glorified (4) daylight

■ *Exercise 11*   **HOMONYMS**

Homonyms are words that sound alike but have different meanings and are spelled differently:

hour, our; some, sum; right, write

When you use homonyms, be sure to write the homonym that expresses the meaning you intend.

DIRECTIONS: Underline the homonym that best completes each sentence.

Example: Don't (<u>stare</u>, stair) at the staggering drunk!

1. Have you decided (weather, whether) you will go or not?
2. The (scene, seen) from the mountaintop is spectacular.
3. You must (great, grate) the potatoes to make hash browns.
4. The teacher will (counsel, council) all students with low grades.
5. Yesterday, the Keystones left (their, there) children at (their, they're) friend's house.
6. Each sentence should begin with a (capitol, capital) letter.
7. The tables and chairs at McDonald's are (stationery, stationary).
8. Why can't lawyers speak (plane, plain) English?
9. The (mail, male) seems to bring only bills!
10. (Your, You're) tax return is ready to be signed.
11. The (principle, principal) of the strike was to gain benefits for (principle, principal) actors and other members of the Screen Actors' Guild.
12. (Steal, Steel) is one of the strongest metals.
13. Jessica should (of, have) called sooner.
14. Eva can't (hear, here) what (your, you're) saying.
15. Clean the windows and mirrors (to, two, too).

EXTRA PRACTICE

Use each of the following words in a sentence.

their	too	hear
you're	principle	steel

You may write a separate sentence for each word or use more than one word in the same sentence.

Answers begin on page 29.

■ *Exercise 12* **WORDS OFTEN CONFUSED**

Certain words are commonly confused because their spellings are similar:

advise (a verb meaning "to counsel")

advice (a noun meaning "a suggestion")

To select the right word, think carefully about the sentence's meaning:

I advised her to follow my advice.

If you are unsure about which word is correct, look up the choices in a dictionary.

> **DIRECTIONS:** Underline the correct word choice in each of the following sentences.

Example: *It was so cold that we could see our (breath, breathe).*

1. Janice gave her room a (thorough, through) cleaning.
2. Father McGuire gives helpful (advice, advise).
3. Please try not to (loose, lose) your homework again.
4. (Where, Were) did you go last night?
5. The experimental drug may (effect, affect) your digestion.
6. He was not (conscience, conscious) of his annoying habit.
7. The directions will tell you how to (proceed, precede).
8. We had eight hours to (accept, except) or reject the offer.
9. For (desert, dessert) there is rice pudding.
10. If you have a question about benefits, contact the (personal, personnel) office.
11. All of the states have tough penalties for the use or sale of (elicit, illicit) drugs.
12. The Griffins wore their best (cloths, clothes) to their son's graduation.
13. You should (bath, bathe) an infant in lukewarm water.

EXTRA PRACTICE

Write sentences using the following words correctly:

advise	quite
clothes	than
loose	personal

You may write a separate sentence for each word or use more than one word in the same sentence. (Check your dictionary if necessary.)

Answers begin on page 29.

Exercise 13   SPELLING REVIEW II

DIRECTIONS: In each set of words, find the misspelled word if there is one. Then blacken the space in the answer grid over the number that corresponds to the misspelled word. If there is no misspelled word, blacken the space numbered (5).

Example: (1) peirce (2) conceive (3) believe (4) seizure

1. (1) textbook (2) bilboard (3) update (4) teacup
2. (1) maxamum (2) minimum (3) premium (4) forum
3. (1) seen (2) redeem (3) extreem (4) theme
4. (1) surgury (2) perjury (3) luxury (4) treasury
5. (1) chastity (2) sanity (3) specialty (4) continueity
6. (1) follow (2) below (3) solo (4) mellow
7. (1) appealling (2) retelling (3) sailing (4) distilling
8. (1) immature (2) import (3) imperial (4) immobile
9. (1) baitted (2) batted (3) hated (4) waited
10. (1) lively (2) lovable (3) valueable (4) agreeable
11. (1) frying (2) fried (3) fries (4) refried
12. (1) hurrying (2) marrying (3) worrysome (4) trying
13. (1) dissect (2) dissaster (3) dissolve (4) diseased
14. (1) affair (2) affraid (3) affected (4) affirmed
15. (1) rooftop (2) sweetheart (3) taxpayer (4) limesstone
16. (1) handfull (2) fulfill (3) refill (4) careful
17. (1) ciggarette (2) pennant (3) personnel (4) luggage
18. (1) cocktail (2) coconut (3) cocaine (4) cocoon
19. (1) grievience (2) inconvenience (3) patience (4) ingredients
20. (1) enforcement (2) arguement (3) enrichment (4) involvement

Answers begin on page 29.

Exercise 14 SPELLING REVIEW III

> **DIRECTIONS:** Check each sentence for spelling errors. If a word is misspelled, cross it out and write the correct spelling above the word. (There is no more than one misspelled word per sentence.) If all words in a sentence are spelled correctly, write *OK* next to the sentence.

weird

Example: Sondra said, "That teacher is wierd."

1. The post office is inconviently located.
2. I haven't recieved any explanation yet for their peculiar behavior.
3. Lorraine and her unfaithful husband have recently separated.
4. After the boy's tragic death, a child phychologist spoke to his grieving classmates.
5. It is both ilegal and immoral to sell alcohol to a minor.
6. I would have prefered to stay home and relax, but Gary dragged me to the miniature golf course.
7. It is finacially unwise to invest all your earnings in lottery tickets.
8. The demonstrators protested noisyly against the proposed incinerator project.
9. I hope your not going to suggest another tedious game of Go Fish.
10. Were in the world are you planning to go dressed in that bizarre outfit?
11. The outdoor wedding was a joyous occasion for all who attended.
12. Meryl begged off early, saying, "I have to get my beuty sleep."
13. My roomate is one of the most intelligent people I know, but her messages to me are full of misspellings.
14. His parents tried to sheild him from the bad influences in his neighborhood.
15. The letter was written on perfumed stationary; reading it gave me a severe headache.

Answers begin on page 29.

Exercise 15   CAPITALIZATION RULES 1–4

Use the following rules to capitalize words correctly.

1) Capitalize the pronoun *I:*

   When *I* earn my diploma, *I*'ll look for a job.

2) Capitalize the first word of a sentence:

   That news show is good. *There* should be more like it.

3) Capitalize people's names:

   Michael Jordan, Debra Sue Kowalski

4) Capitalize job and family titles when they immediately precede a person's name and are considered to be part of the name:

   Senator Jones and *Aunt* Sarah were high school sweethearts.

   Also capitalize job and family titles when they take the place of a person's name. (If a name could be inserted in place of the title, it is taking the place of a person's name):

   "Come quickly, *Nurse*," cried the *doctor.*

   (A name could be inserted in place of *Nurse* but not in place of *doctor.*)

DIRECTIONS: Check each of the following sentences for capitalization errors. If there is an error, circle the word and write it correctly above. If there is no error, write *OK* next to the sentence.

She

Example: *The author of the book is Alice Walker.* (she) *is one of my favorite writers.*

1. Is Doctor Cotter a child Psychologist?
2. When Congressman Yates arrives, tell him that (ms). Bain called.
3. Why have I got so many bills to pay? I owe money to my dentist, my lawyer, and my landlord.
4. Your aunt, your Uncle, and Grandpa Joe are here.
5. Why is it that when i'm working there's never enough time to visit my grandmother? Perhaps I should learn to schedule my time better.
6. A Doctor spoke to Mayor Daley and Cardinal Bernardin about the local infant mortality rate.
7. Let's go to Mary Lou's! her husband works the late shift tonight, so she may be lonely.

Answers begin on page 29.

■ *Exercise 16*   CAPITALIZATION RULES 5–8

5) Capitalize geographic names and most words derived from them:

People's Republic of *China, Chinese* chef

Some words derived from geographic names are not capitalized:

turkish towel, *roman* numeral, *manila* envelope

Check a dictionary if you are unsure whether to capitalize a word.

6) Capitalize the names of streets, parts of town, and regions of the country:

Martin Luther King Drive, the *West Side*, the *Southwest*

Do not capitalize *north, south, east,* and *west* when used as directions:

The car was headed *west.*

7) Capitalize the names of important buildings and structures:

the *Lincoln Memorial*, the *Empire State Building*

8) Capitalize the names of historic events and periods:

World War I, the *Middle Ages*

DIRECTIONS: Check the sentences below for capitalization errors. Put three underscores under any letter that should be capitalized.

Example: *The john hancock building is on chicago's lakefront.*

1. Does aunt barbara still live in las vegas, nevada?

2. thomas jefferson lived at monticello, his home in virginia.

3. I grew up in the midwest but went to college in the east.

4. My friend darius, the crazy new yorker, lives in manhattan near the george washington bridge.

5. Anita, a professor at the university of georgia in athens, says many northerners go to school in the south.

6. in san francisco, I took a cable car to post street.

7. Whenever cousin edward eats italian food, he recalls the days he spent in milan, italy, during world war II.

EXTRA PRACTICE

Write each of the following, using capital letters correctly:

1. the name of your city or town and your state

2. your favorite ethnic food, such as Japanese food

3. the name of an important building in your city or town

Answers begin on page 29.

■ *Exercise 17*   CAPITALIZATION RULES 9-12

9) Capitalize the brand names of products:

   Puffs tissues, *Sanka*

10) Capitalize the names of companies, stores, banks, etc.:

   the *Shell Oil Company*, the *First National Bank*

11) Capitalize the names of specific organizations:

   the *American Heart Association*

12) Capitalize the names of political parties:

   Democrats, the *Citizens' Community Party*

DIRECTIONS: Check the following sentences for capitalization errors. Put three underscores under any letter that should be capitalized.

Example: *The coca-cola company distributes sprite.*

1. The republicans have many wealthy supporters in large companies such as the xerox corporation.

2. The democrats gained seats in the House, while the republicans gained seats in the Senate.

3. The main offices of the united steel workers are in Pittsburgh.

4. To lose weight, Julie took dexatrim and joined weight watchers.

5. Call the better business bureau, and see if the charitable organization is registered.

6. Anita is active in the girl scouts of america.

7. My favorite cereal, rice krispies, is made by kellogg's, whose national headquarters are in Battle Creek, Michigan.

EXTRA PRACTICE

Write each of the following, using capital letters correctly:

1. the brand name of the shampoo you use

2. the name of a store in your city

3. the name of your governor's political party

Answers begin on page 30.

■ *Exercise 18*   CAPITALIZATION RULES 13–16

13) In general, capitalize specific names but not general names:

   high school, *Worcester East High School;* taxi service, *American Taxi Service*

14) Capitalize names of specific school courses but not names of a general subject area unless it is a language:

   algebra, *Algebra I;* auto mechanics, *Auto Mechanics 29B;* English, *English Literature 102*

15) Capitalize the names of languages, religions, and religious denominations:

   Italian, Spanish, Judaism, Baptist

16) Capitalize all names referring to God, a deity, or a worshipped figure:

   Christ, Allah, Krishna

DIRECTIONS: Check the following sentences for capitalization errors. Put three underscores under any letter that should be capitalized.

Example: After graduating from high school, I attended parker college.

1. would a presbyterian view religious holidays differently from a catholic?

2. if you took high school math, you should be ready for mathematics 101 in college.

3. uncle carl and aunt helga are close friends with professor rappaport, who teaches russian at a community college in my state.

4. the auto mechanic at midas told me he had learned his trade at the andrew jackson vocational school.

5. cynthia is studying computer science at the national institute of technology.

6. dr. mustafa azawi is an expert on islamic law and the koran.

7. if you join the jazz band, you'll get credit for music appreciation 201.

8. my favorite class is called latin american literature in the twentieth century; it is taught by a professor from colombia. we read the books in spanish, but classes are conducted in english.

9. the rabbi spoke of god and read in hebrew from the torah.

10. my uncle in korea took me to several buddhist temples.

Answers begin on page 30.

■ *Exercise 19* CAPITALIZATION 1–16 REVIEW

DIRECTIONS: Check each of the following sentences for capitalization errors. If there is a mistake, blacken the space over the number corresponding to it in the answer grid. If there is no error, blacken the space numbered (5).

Example: I prefer Doctor Stein to the Doctor that my father sees.
     1   2   3   4

○ ○ ● ○ ○
1 2 3 4 5

1. Does American Airlines fly to Hawaii? I would like to visit
        1   2   3
several Islands there.
        4

1. ○ ○ ○ ○ ○
   1 2 3 4 5

2. We visited the Sistine chapel in the Vatican when we
                 1   2   3
were in Italy.
        4

2. ○ ○ ○ ○ ○
   1 2 3 4 5

3. The Gibson company donated an exquisite collection of
           1
Nigerian art to the city's largest museum.
   2   3   4

3. ○ ○ ○ ○ ○
   1 2 3 4 5

4. During the great Depression, President Franklin Roosevelt
                1   2
instituted government programs to help the unemployed.
           3   4

4. ○ ○ ○ ○ ○
   1 2 3 4 5

5. The Mississippi River is the longest River in the country.
        1   2   3   4

5. ○ ○ ○ ○ ○
   1 2 3 4 5

6. In 1988, United States citizens elected a Republican
                 1   2
president but a largely democratic Congress.
  3   4

6. ○ ○ ○ ○ ○
   1 2 3 4 5

7. Drive South on the Indiana Tollway to East Oak Avenue.
         1   2   3   4

7. ○ ○ ○ ○ ○
   1 2 3 4 5

8. A Mother does not always win full custody of her child,
     1
especially if the father impresses a judge with his
                 2   3
eagerness to be the custodial parent.
                              4

8. ○ ○ ○ ○ ○
   1 2 3 4 5

9. During the Revolutionary War, the colonists fought the
                           1   2
British with some aid from the french.
  3   4

9. ○ ○ ○ ○ ○
   1 2 3 4 5

10. The Spot Welding I Class meets in the vocational building
            1   2   3
on Lennox Avenue.
          4

10. ○ ○ ○ ○ ○
    1 2 3 4 5

Answers begin on page 31.

Exercise 20 CAPITALIZATION RULES 17–18

17) Capitalize abbreviated titles after a name:

John Marks, *Sr.*; William James, *Ph.D.*

> **Note:** The first letter in the abbreviation is capitalized, as well as each letter immediately following a period.

18) Capitalize the first and last words in titles and all the important words in between:

The Grapes of *Wrath; One* from the *Heart*

> **Note:** Words like *a, an, the, of, and, from,* and *to* are not capitalized unless they are the first or last word in a title.

DIRECTIONS: Write each sentence below on the blank that follows it. Insert capital letters as needed, using rules 1–18.

Example: well, maestro, did you enjoy beethoven's fifth symphony?

Well, Maestro, did you enjoy Beethoven's Fifth Symphony?

1. did you see *a nightmare on elm street* when it first came out?

2. we sang "we shall overcome" in memory of dr. martin luther king, jr.

3. the book *a night to remember* is about the sinking of the titanic.

4. my cousin, al morales, m.d., referred me to you, doctor.

5. my favorite mystery by p. d. james is *a taste for death.*

6. last night we watched *from here to eternity,* a movie about world war II.

7. when the concorde takes off for europe, general stone, u.s.a.f., will be aboard.

8. *west side story* is loosely based on shakespeare's *romeo and juliet.*

EXTRA PRACTICE

Using capital letters correctly, write the title of your favorite movie, book, and song.

Answers begin on page 31.

Exercise 21   CAPITALIZATION RULES 19–22

19) Capitalize the names of holidays:

Columbus Day, the *Fourth* of *July*

20) Capitalize the names of the days of the week:

Sunday, Wednesday

21) Capitalize the names of the months:

September, May

Do not capitalize the seasons of the year:

fall, winter, spring, summer

22) Capitalize the abbreviations B.C. and A.D.

DIRECTIONS: Check the sentences below for capitalization errors. Put three underscores under any letter that should be capitalized.

Example: *is labor day always the first monday in september?*

1. our anniversary, may 28, sometimes falls on memorial day.

2. macy's is open late on monday and thursday evenings.

3. florists always look forward to February 14, valentine's day.

4. we always celebrate thanksgiving on the fourth thursday in november.

5. the coins are believed to date back to somewhere between 50 b.c. and a.d. 100.

6. the office will be closed thursday and friday because we must take the monthly inventory.

7. every thirty days, more or less, we begin a new month.

8. i can never remember if halloween is on october 30 or october 31.

9. the months that have thirty days are september, april, june, and november.

10. the employees want to take the holiday on monday or friday, which would extend their weekend to three days.

Answers begin on page 31.

■ *Exercise 22*   **CAPITALIZATION RULE 23**

23) In a letter, capitalize each word of the opening greeting except *and:*

Dear Mr. and *Mrs. Michaels*

Capitalize the first word of the closing:

Your devoted fan; *Sincerely* yours

DIRECTIONS: Check the letter below for capitalization errors. Put three underscores under any letter that should be capitalized.

---

february 6, 199—

Mr. Jacob hargreaves
Perfect cookbooks, inc.
1946 Elm ave.
Chicago, Illinois 60600

Dear mr. Hargreaves:

    In november, i ordered a set of your cookbooks, which i had seen advertised in *ladies' home journal.* it is now february, and i have not received any of the books. I couldn't even use the recipes i especially wanted for christmas cookies and fruitcake!

    if you cannot guarantee that i'll have the books in six weeks—no later than march 15—please return my check. I hope to use the easter cake decorating tips i read about, so i must have the books next month.

sincerely,
estelle Louis
Howe Park Bake shoppe

Answers begin on page 31.

■ *Exercise 23* CAPITALIZATION RULE 24

A **direct quotation** uses quotation marks ("...") to identify the speaker's exact words or thoughts.

24) Capitalize the first word in a direct quotation:

"It's time to go," explained Malcolm.

As she sat down, she thought, *"It's* great to be alive."

If a direct quotation is interrupted or divided, the second part of the quotation begins with a capital letter when a new sentence starts:

"Don't worry," said the lawyer. *"We* have plenty of solid evidence."

"Yesterday," explained the utility representative, *"was* when the payment was due."

Notice that *was* does not begin a new sentence, so it does not need to be capitalized.

DIRECTIONS: All capitalization has been omitted in the following story. Put three underscores under any letter that should be capitalized.

---

stephen smith lay in bed at monroe hospital, his mother by his side. "my son," wept mrs. smith, "was shot for wearing the wrong thing, and that's all."

on wednesday, june 10, mr. smith was shot while waiting for a bus on oak street near harbor drive. he was wearing a purple scarf with his blue windbreaker. "i didn't realize," he said later, "that those were the colors of the majestic knights or that i was on the turf of the green demons."

a passerby, jacklyn michaels, told the *daily news,* "as the attackers drove off, i saw them making gang signals." ms. michaels, a medical student at leland university, immediately shouted for help and began first aid. chong dae park, a korean immigrant who had arrived in the city only the previous saturday, heard her cries and called 911 from a nearby pay phone. "please send help!" he told the dispatcher. "a man is shot near burger king on oak street."

mr. park and ms. michaels later joined stephen's mother at the hospital, where the doctor made an announcement. "i have good news," said dr. vega. "this young man will be home in time to celebrate independence day with his family on july 4!"

Answers begin on page 32.

■ *Exercise 24*   CAPITALIZATION 1–24 REVIEW

> **DIRECTIONS:** Check each of the following sentences for capitalization errors. If there is a mistake, blacken the space over the number corresponding to it in the answer grid. If there is no error, blacken the space numbered (5).

Example: After one week's vacation in June, I am really ready to
enjoy the Summer.

1 2 3 ● 5
1 2 3 4 5

1. Rabbi Meyer and reverend O'Neil led the interfaith
Thanksgiving service at Wheadon Church.

   1. ○ ○ ○ ○ ○
   1 2 3 4 5

2. The classic horror film *The Phantom of the Opera* is still
popular.

   2. ○ ○ ○ ○ ○
   1 2 3 4 5

3. "You must move your car," warned the officer, "Or it will
be towed away."

   3. ○ ○ ○ ○ ○
   1 2 3 4 5

4. The winter months, especially January, are often
depressing to people who live in the midwest.

   4. ○ ○ ○ ○ ○
   1 2 3 4 5

5. Is it legal for a United States Senator to be the
spokesperson for a European company?

   5. ○ ○ ○ ○ ○
   1 2 3 4 5

6. "Is Geritol considered a vitamin?" asked Dawn. Bob
replied, "no, it's a mixture of vitamins and minerals."

   6. ○ ○ ○ ○ ○
   1 2 3 4 5

7. Getting up her courage, Yolanda said, "Well, Doctor,
perhaps I should see another Doctor for a second
opinion."

   7. ○ ○ ○ ○ ○
   1 2 3 4 5

8. Although she has lived in this country for three years,
Mrs. Kebede still speaks only Amharic, the language of
her native Ethiopia.

   8. ○ ○ ○ ○ ○
   1 2 3 4 5

9. The Principal asked if we would like to meet
Ms. Johnson, his assistant.

   9. ○ ○ ○ ○ ○
   1 2 3 4 5

10. "Stop working now," <u>o</u>rdered the monitor. "<u>Y</u>our time on
₁ ₂
the <u>Science section</u> was up at 11:00 A.M."
₃ ₄

10. ○ ○ ○ ○ ○
   1 2 3 4 5

11. "Wait a minute!" <u>S</u>houted the <u>s</u>tudent. "<u>L</u>et me have time
₁ ₂ ₃
to mark one last answer. <u>OK</u>?"
₄

11. ○ ○ ○ ○ ○
   1 2 3 4 5

12. On the <u>West coast</u>, <u>J</u>apanese cars, such as Nissans, may
₁ ₂ ₃
be less <u>e</u>xpensive than in the <u>East</u>.
₄

12. ○ ○ ○ ○ ○
   1 2 3 4 5

13. We saw the Spike Lee <u>m</u>ovie *Do <u>The</u> Right Thing* at our
₁ ₂
<u>n</u>eighborhood <u>t</u>heater.
₃ ₄

13. ○ ○ ○ ○ ○
   1 2 3 4 5

14. The United Auto Workers asked General Motors
<u>C</u>orporation to reopen the <u>Winter contract</u> negotiations in
₁ ₂ ₃
the <u>Midwest</u>.
₄

14. ○ ○ ○ ○ ○
   1 2 3 4 5

15. "Learn your <u>Math</u> now," warned the <u>high school</u> teacher,
₁ ₂ ₃
"<u>o</u>r you will never make it in Basic Accounting I at
₄
college."

15. ○ ○ ○ ○ ○
   1 2 3 4 5

16. "Becoming a <u>g</u>eologist is very important to Serena, my
₁
<u>N</u>iece," explained <u>A</u>unt Reyna, "so she'll be moving to
₂ ₃
the <u>Southwest</u> in a few weeks."
₄

16. ○ ○ ○ ○ ○
   1 2 3 4 5

17. "On a closely related issue," began <u>S</u>peaker of the <u>House</u>
₁ ₂
Tom Foley, "<u>T</u>he bill regarding <u>c</u>hild care is now up for
₃ ₄
discussion."

17. ○ ○ ○ ○ ○
   1 2 3 4 5

18. Seven-Up, a soft <u>d</u>rink, is owned by the Philip Morris
₁
<u>C</u>ompany, a large <u>t</u>obacco <u>C</u>ompany.
₂ ₃ ₄

18. ○ ○ ○ ○ ○
   1 2 3 4 5

19. My best <u>f</u>riend Delia, who lives in the <u>n</u>orthwestern part
₁ ₂
of our <u>c</u>ontinent, believes that clean, moist air is what
₃
keeps her so healthy. <u>d</u>on't you agree?
₄

19. ○ ○ ○ ○ ○
   1 2 3 4 5

20. As the <u>Worshippers</u> neared <u>Mecca</u>, they began to give
₁ ₂
thanks to <u>M</u>ohammed with a prayer from the <u>Koran</u>.
₃ ₄

20. ○ ○ ○ ○ ○
   1 2 3 4 5

Answers begin on page 32.

28

■ ANSWER KEY

EXERCISE 1
1. com/mu/ni/ty
2. en/vi/ron/ment
3. li/quor
4. ath/lete
5. in/sti/tu/tion
6. tem/per/a/ture
7. to/mor/row
8. com/mit/ted
9. dif/fer/ent
10. priv/i/lege
11. gov/ern/ment
12. jew/el/ry

EXERCISE 2
1. convenient
2. presentation
3. combination
4. OK
5. exactly
6. unusual
7. responsible
8. irrelevant
9. advantages
10. explain
11. lawyer
12. library
13. furniture
14. OK
15. economical

EXERCISE 3
1. 3
2. 3
3. 2
4. 1
5. 5
6. 2
7. 1
8. 3
9. 2
10. 1
11. 5
12. 1
13. 2
14. 3
15. 2

EXERCISE 4
1. neighbor's
2. relief
3. perceive
4. mischief
5. receiver
6. piece
7. OK
8. sieges

EXERCISE 5
1. 2
2. 5
3. 3
4. 1
5. 5
6. 3
7. 2
8. 5
9. 2
10. 2
11. 4
12. 2
13. 1
14. 3

EXERCISE 6
1. weekend
2. roommate
3. heavyweight
4. barroom
5. shareholder
6. reincarnation
7. mismanage
8. preregister
9. prorated
10. inconvenient
11. unfold
12. illegible
13. supersonic
14. semimonthly
15. irregular
1. OK
2. bookkeeper
3. OK
4. OK
5. headstrong
6. OK
7. dissatisfied
8. immaterial
9. reemploy
10. OK
11. OK
12. inedible
13. OK
14. OK
15. irrelevant

EXERCISE 7
1. annoys
2. finely
3. blameless
4. attaches
5. flies
6. craziness
7. payment
8. plentiful
9. resists
10. painfully
1. OK
2. babies
3. commitment
4. truly
5. OK
6. fries
7. argument
8. OK
9. worries
10. watches

EXERCISE 8
1. listener
2. tried
3. desirable
4. trapped
5. revealed
6. sleepier
7. annoyance
8. biodegradable
9. sloppiest
10. expelled
11. advantageous
12. limited

EXERCISE 9
1. seems, hurrying
2. wondered, sadness
3. ladies, daintily, sipped
4. OK, enabling
5. OK, walking, OK
6. plays, toys, excited, racing, cars
7. truly, likely, commitment
8. sincerely, OK, OK, remarks, OK

29

EXERCISE 10

1. 3   11. 3
2. 5   12. 4
3. 1   13. 2
4. 4   14. 3
5. 3   15. 1
6. 3   16. 2
7. 3   17. 3
8. 5   18. 2
9. 1   19. 2
10. 3

EXERCISE 11

1. whether   9. mail
2. scene   10. Your
3. grate   11. principle; principal
4. counsel   12. Steel
5. their; their   13. have
6. capital   14. hear; you're
7. stationary   15. too
8. plain

EXERCISE 12

1. thorough   8. accept
2. advice   9. dessert
3. lose   10. personnel
4. Where   11. illicit
5. affect   12. clothes
6. conscious   13. bathe
7. proceed

EXERCISE 13

1. 2   11. 5
2. 1   12. 3
3. 3   13. 2
4. 1   14. 2
5. 4   15. 4
6. 5   16. 1
7. 1   17. 1
8. 5   18. 5
9. 1   19. 1
10. 3   20. 2

EXERCISE 14

1. inconveniently   9. you're
2. received   10. Where
3. OK   11. OK
4. psychologist   12. beauty
5. illegal   13. roommate
6. preferred   14. shield
7. financially   15. stationery
8. noisily

EXERCISE 15

1. psychologist   5. I'm
2. Ms.   6. doctor
3. OK   7. Her
4. uncle

EXERCISE 16

1. Does aunt barbara still live in las vegas, nevada?

2. thomas jefferson lived at monticello, his home in virginia.

3. I grew up in the midwest but went to college in the east.

4. My friend darius, the crazy new yorker, lives in manhattan near the george washington bridge.

5. Anita, a professor at the university of georgia in athens, says many northerners go to school in the south.

6. in san francisco, I took a cable car to post street.

7. Whenever cousin edward eats italian food, he recalls the days he spent in milan, italy, during world war II.

EXERCISE 17

1. The republicans have many wealthy supporters in large companies such as the xerox corporation.

2. The democrats gained seats in the House, while the republicans gained seats in the Senate.

3. The main offices of the united steel workers are in Pittsburgh.

4. To lose weight, Julie took dexatrim and joined weight watchers.

5. Call the better business bureau, and see if the charitable organization is registered.

6. Anita is active in the girl scouts of america.

7. My favorite cereal, rice krispies, is made by kellogg's, whose national headquarters are in Battle Creek, Michigan.

EXERCISE 18

1. would a presbyterian view religious holidays differently from a catholic?

2. if you took high school math, you should be ready for mathematics 101 in college.

3. uncle carl and aunt helga are close friends with professor rappaport, who teaches russian at a community college in my state.

4. the auto mechanic at midas told me he had learned his trade at the andrew jackson vocational school.

5. cynthia is studying computer science at the national institute of technology.

6. dr. mustafa azawi is an expert on islamic law and the koran.

7. if you join the jazz band, you'll get credit for music appreciation 201.

8. my favorite class is called latin american literature in the twentieth century; it is taught by a professor from colombia. we read the books in spanish, but classes are conducted in english.

9. the rabbi spoke of god and read in hebrew from the torah.

10. my uncle in korea took me to several buddhist temples.

EXERCISE 19

1. 4	6. 4
2. 2	7. 1
3. 1	8. 1
4. 1	9. 4
5. 3	10. 2

EXERCISE 20

1. Did you see *A Nightmare on Elm Street* when it first came out?
2. We sang "We Shall Overcome" in memory of Dr. Martin Luther King, Jr.
3. The book *A Night to Remember* is about the sinking of the Titanic.
4. My cousin, Al Morales, M.D., referred me to you, Doctor.
5. My favorite mystery by P. D. James is *A Taste for Death.*
6. Last night we watched *From Here to Eternity,* a movie about World War II.
7. When the Concorde takes off for Europe, General Stone, U.S.A.F., will be aboard.
8. *West Side Story* is loosely based on Shakespeare's *Romeo and Juliet.*

EXERCISE 21

1. our anniversary, may 28, sometimes falls on memorial day.
2. macy's is open late on monday and thursday evenings.
3. florists always look forward to February 14, valentine's day.
4. we always celebrate thanksgiving on the fourth thursday in november.
5. the coins are believed to date back to somewhere between 50 b.c. and a.d. 100.
6. the office will be closed thursday and friday because we must take the monthly inventory.
7. every thirty days, more or less, we begin a new month.
8. i can never remember if halloween is on october 30 or october 31.
9. the months that have thirty days are september, april, june, and november.
10. the employees want to take the holiday on monday or friday, which would extend their weekend to three days.

EXERCISE 22

february 6, 199—

Mr. Jacob hargreaves

Perfect cookbooks, inc.

1946 Elm ave.

Chicago, Illinois 60600

Dear mr. Hargreaves:

In november, i ordered a set of your cookbooks, which i had seen advertised in *ladies' home journal.* it is now february, and i have not received any of the books. I couldn't even use the recipes i especially wanted for christmas cookies and fruitcake!

if you cannot guarantee that i'll have the books in six weeks—no later than march 15—please return my check. I hope to use the easter cake decorating tips i read about, so i must have the books next month.

sincerely,

estelle Louis

Howe Park Bake shoppe

EXERCISE 23

stephen smith lay in bed at monroe hospital, his mother by his side. "my son," wept mrs. smith, "was shot for wearing the wrong thing, and that's all."

on wednesday, june 10, mr. smith was shot while waiting for a bus on oak street near harbor drive. he was wearing a purple scarf with his blue windbreaker. "i didn't realize," he said later, "that those were the colors of the majestic knights or that i was on the turf of the green demons."

a passerby, jacklyn michaels, told the *daily news*, "as the attackers drove off, i saw them making gang signals." ms. michaels, a medical student at leland university, immediately shouted for help and began first aid. chong dae park, a korean immigrant who had arrived in the city only the previous saturday, heard her cries and called 911 from a nearby pay phone. "please send help!" he told the dispatcher. "a man is shot near burger king on oak street."

mr. park and ms. michaels later joined stephen's mother at the hospital, where the doctor made an announcement. "i have good news," said dr. vega. "this young man will be home in time to celebrate independence day with his family on july 4!"

EXERCISE 24

1.	1	11.	1
2.	5	12.	2
3.	4	13.	2
4.	4	14.	2
5.	1	15.	1
6.	4	16.	2
7.	4	17.	3
8.	5	18.	4
9.	1	19.	4
10.	3	20.	1

Available only in packages of 10. To order, use number 3743-1.

CONTEMPORARY BOOKS

a division of NTC/Contemporary Publishing Company

90000

9 780809 237456

ISBN 0-8092-3745-8